CW00457687

Tantra of the Tachikawa Ryu

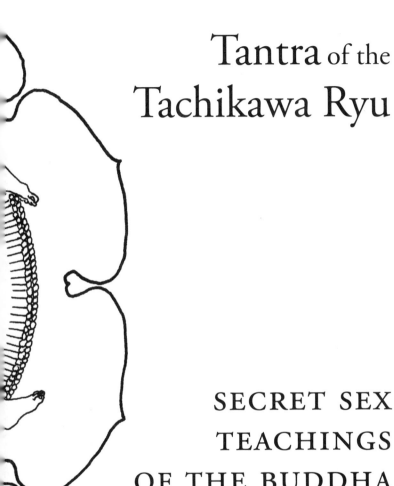

Tantra of the Tachikawa Ryu

SECRET SEX TEACHINGS OF THE BUDDHA

John Stevens

STONE BRIDGE PRESS • *Berkeley, California*

Published by
Stone Bridge Press
P.O. Box 8208
Berkeley, CA 94707
TEL 510-524-8732 • sbp@stonebridge.com • www.stonebridge.com

Cover and title-page illustration by Colin Stevens; the character in the center is **A**, a Sanskrit seed-syllable of Dainichi Nyorai (Great Sun Buddha), representing the unity of all existence.

Interior illustrations supplied by the author.

Text © 2010 John Stevens.

First edition 2010.

Cover and text design by Linda Ronan.

Printed in the United States of America.

2015 2014 2013 2012 2011 2010   10 9 8 7 6 5 4 3 2 1

LIBRARY OF CONGRESS CATALOGING-IN-PUBLICATION DATA
Stevens, John, 1947–
   Tantra of the Tachikawa Ryu : secret sex teachings of the Buddha / John
Stevens. — 1st ed.
      p. cm.
   ISBN 978-1-933330-88-4
   1. Tachikawa School—Doctrines. 2. Sex—Religious aspects—Tantric
Buddhism. 3. Hotoke Gozen, 1160?–1180?—Fiction. I. Title.
   BQ8854.S74 2010
   294.3'925—dc22
                                                    2010029249

*The union of Yin and Yang brings a couple
to perfection;
Meditation within sexual congress is the
supreme law of sages.
Selfless glory is the true bliss;
In real sex this very body becomes Buddha!*

HOTOKE HAD BEEN very fond of her late *danna* (patron) Hidemune. He had ransomed her from the pleasure quarters, paid off her contract, for which she would be eternally grateful. She had been sold to the brothel when she was just six years of age by her indigent parents, poor farmers from the frozen north of Japan. Her debt to the house was not small, and Hidemune had paid a small fortune to secure her release.

Hotoke was the star courtesan of the house, and the madam was reluctant to let her go. (That added to the ransom price.) She had extraordinary beauty—large wide eyes, a clear complexion, a perfectly proportioned melon-shaped face, a long elegant neck, a supple yet delicate body, and graceful demeanor. She seemed to have all the thirty-two marks of a divine being and was given the name Hotoke, "Buddha," because she brought infinite bliss to anyone who gazed on her lovely form. (In contrast, one of her renowned predecessors assumed the name "Hell," because her beauty was so fatally alluring.)

Hidemune was not the one who performed Hotoke's

mizu-age, the "deflowering ceremony," when she was age thirteen—that deed was done by a wealthy old merchant who only liked virgins. Hotoke had a number of clients prior to Hidemune and a brief, secret affair with one of the houseboys. The sex with the young man was fun and exciting—they both would have been severely punished if caught in the act—but it took place furtively in the dark corners of the building. The infatuation was soon over.

Hidemune was her favorite, however. In fact, he was everyone's favorite because of his generous spirit and his insatiable appetite for sex. He was a provincial lord, about fifty years of age, and spent nearly every night at the pleasure quarters when he was in Edo. Hidemune loved sex but not drunken, hasty, rough, or perverted sex like most of the other guests. What he wanted was sex that required refinement, quality, and stamina. Hidemune drank and ate comparatively little, and that gave him more energy for his amorous pursuits. He was a clever poet and a talented calligrapher. As was the fashion, many of the girls had him brush something appropriate directly on their kimono. For Hotoke, he had written the character for "Buddha" on the top of her sash. Hotoke later found out that he knew the tea ceremony and was a connoisseur of fine art. It was also rumored that Hidemune was a student of one of the famous Yagyu swordsmen. Hotoke did not know if this was true but she certainly felt that, on occasion, Hidemune had a steely, hard edge to him.

It is the dream of every girl in the pleasure quarters

to be ransomed by someone like Hidemune, but Hotoke never thought it would happen. Suddenly, one day Hidemune announced that he had paid off her contract. He was setting her up in a district where many samurai lords kept their lady companions, either as wives or concubines.

While most of the clients still continued to visit the pleasure quarters even after they had a permanent partner, Hidemune stopped completely and spent his nights only with Hotoke when he was in town. He liked to have her play the koto and sing for him. Often Hidemune would prepare tea. The smell of the fresh green tea and its pungent, astringent taste was, for Hotoke, extremely erotic and stimulating. Their love-making was slow and long lasting.

Oral sex was frowned upon in the pleasure quarters, for obscure reasons, and Hidemune never asked for it when Hotoke was there, but once she was free he introduced her to that delightful practice, known as "playing the flute" (when a man received it) and "sipping the mountain stream" (when a woman received it). When it was done simultaneously it was called "feeding crows."

Hidemune's favorite positions for intercourse were "raging tiger" (both with their knees up), "the clinch" (his legs wrapped tightly around hers), "wild camellia" (she facing front perched on his jade stalk), "rowing from the rear" (from behind, she kneeling, he standing), and the old mainstays "mandarin ducks moving their tails" (face to face, he on top) and "tea-grinder" (she on top in various permutations). Hidemune liked to bathe with Hotoke;

sometimes they made love standing up or in the water with her sitting on the edge of the tub.

Hidemune liked to sleep together with Hotoke, both naked, in the same bedding. This was unusual for most couples; they usually wore some type of bed clothes and slept on separate futons. However, Hidemune told Hotoke, "I want to absorb your vibrant energy," and held her next to him through the night.

During the day, Hotoke would practice tea ceremony, calligraphy, and the koto. Life was good for her. Alas, even though Hidemune seemed in excellent health when he last visited her, one morning a courier from his domain appeared.

"I'm sorry to inform you that Lord Hidemune has passed away. He left this bundle for you." The courier departed before Hotoke could ask what happened. She never found out.

Inside the wrapped bundle she found a good measure of gold coins. There was a sheet of calligraphy that had the large character *ku*, meaning "emptiness." She remembered that Hidemune once said to her, "All things are empty— that is the first and primary teaching of Buddhism."

IT HAD BEEN a year since Hidemune had passed away. So Hotoke wanted to hold a short memorial service for him at the simple home altar she had set up in the main room of her house. In that neighborhood, people usually asked the priests of Kongo-ji, a nearby Shingon temple, to conduct the service. Hotoke made the arrangements, and a priest from Kongo-ji was to come in a week.

Since Kakusho, the abbot of Kongo-ji, was busy that day, he instructed his attendant Dai-en to go. Dai-en was the third son of a large family, and, as was the custom, he was given to a temple as an acolyte. Like Hotoke, he was just six years old when he left his family. The monks had raised him.

Dai-en was serious about his monastic vows, unlike most of the other monks. They either snuck out at night to head for the pleasure quarters—disguised as "doctors," who also had shaved heads—or they played among themselves. Legend had it that the founder of their school, Kobo Daishi, was the one who had introduced homosexuality into Japan, and so they saw no sin in such behavior. Dai-en had been dragged once to the pleasure quarters by some of the senior monks, and although it was a pleasant experience—the courtesan was kind and understanding; the monks said her name was Kannon, "Goddess of Compassion"—Dai-en was too shy and unsure of himself to enjoy it much.

The week before the memorial service, Hotoke found herself having mesmerizing erotic dreams. As a courtesan and concubine, she had never had such dreams. Although she had not had contact with a man for over a year, that suited her fine, she thought—she had been with enough men to last a lifetime. Suddenly, however, she felt aroused all the time. She was, after all, only in her late twenties and in good health. Was Hidemune contacting her from beyond the grave?

Dai-en arrived at the house at the scheduled time. He was stunned by Hotoke's beauty, even though she was dressed in a formal black mourning kimono and wearing no cosmetics. As she led the monk inside, Hotoke became excited. He was not the frail, wrinkled old abbot she had expected but a young and handsome monk.

Dai-en kindled the incense, and they situated themselves before the altar in a gesture of prayer, their folded hands ringed with a rosary. Dai-en began to chant. His voice was rich and clear; he was proud of his ability to recite the scriptures. However, to his alarm and surprise, he had a painfully hard erection. This had never happened before, and even an increase in the fervor of his prayers had no effect.

Hotoke was similarly affected. Her magic pearl (clitoris) was throbbing, and she could not keep her mind on the service. She had lost control. Without a word, Hotoke stood in front of Dai-en. She parted his robes, liberated his little buddha (penis) from all the layers of clothing, lifted her kimono, and sat on top of him. Dai-en was still kneeling, so he leaned back on the mat and braced himself with both hands.

Hotoke was so aroused she went off, with a muffled cry, as soon as his little buddha entered her jade gate. Dai-en followed quickly—he could not hold back. He rolled her over and began to thrust wildly. Hotoke let him do so for a bit and then got on top again—she needed to be in charge. Hotoke ground her hips against his little buddha for a short time and then shivered with delight. Dai-en released another stream of sperm inside her. They were in the Pure Land.

Hotoke got off, silently redid her disheveled hair, and put her clothes back together. Dai-en, who had been divested of all his robes, picked them up and rearranged them in the proper form. Neither had said a word during the entire incident. They sat before the altar, made a prostration, and then bowed to each other.

Hotoke had prepared some refreshments in the next room. Dai-en, whose head was spinning, managed to drink the tea and eat one of the sweet cakes. Other than "Please help yourself," Hotoke said nothing, but she had a slight, beatific smile on her face.

"I must be going," Dai-en said, excusing himself. Hotoke showed him out, saying, "Thank you so much for coming. I hope to see you again soon." She presented him with a donation envelope.

WHEN DAI-EN RETURNED to Kongo-ji, Kakusho summoned him to the abbot's quarters. Dai-en was terrified. He had witnessed Kakusho's ability to read other people's minds. It was not a rumor—the abbot was able to discern a falsehood immediately. There was no way for Dai-en to dissemble. The abbot would find him out, and Dai-en would, he feared, be expelled from the monastery.

When Kakusho asked how the service went, Dai-en replied honestly, "I had sex with Lady Hotoke."

"I know. I can see it on your face," the abbot replied quietly. "Other monks would have concocted a lie, but you told me the truth. If you had gone there to seduce her or impulsively forced yourself on her, that would be a great sin, and I would evict you immediately from the temple. However, she needed someone to quell her passions, and you helped put her at ease. The use of passion to liberate a person in distress is permitted in our school. We are to take compassion on everyone."

Dai-en was dumbstruck.

Kakusho asked, "Have you heard of the Tachikawa Ryu?"

"I know the name," Dai-en said. "It was a heretical teaching that was banned."

"The Tachikawa Ryu was outlawed by the authorities," Kakusho began in a serious tone, "but never completely suppressed. It went underground and still exists. One of the founders was a monk from our school named Monkan. He was an exemplary monk in every way: for years he faithfully kept the precepts, read every volume of the Buddhist canon, meditated for months on end, debated with the most learned scholars, and subsisted on meager fare. Still, nothing could quench his inner fire, the desire for passionate love. One night, a beautiful woman appeared to Monkan in a vision and said, 'In order to experience the Great Bliss, a man and woman have to unite. Liberation can only be realized through the act of sexual love.' Monkan went on to realize this truth after experimenting with a series of partners and applying various techniques. His teachings became very popular. Problems arose, however. Although the teachings of the Tachikawa Ryu are potent and very effective, they are extremely dangerous. Too many people were misusing them, and that is why the sect was suppressed. I am in sympathy with the aims of the Tachikawa Ryu and its methods but only for those who are sincere and with self-control."

Kakusho got up, went into an inner room, and brought back a short text.

"I want you to copy this and think about the contents as you write each character," he instructed Dai-en.

The text was entitled:

The Sutra Proclaiming the Secret Method
Enabling a Man and Woman to Experience
the Bliss of Buddhahood in This Very Body

And this is what Dai-en read:

———

The Tachikawa Ryu Holy-of-Holies: The jewel in the lotus.

Sexual intercourse between a man and a woman is the supreme Buddha activity. Sex is the source of intense pleasure, the root of creation, necessary for every living being, and a natural act of veneration. To be united as a man and a woman is to be united with Buddha. Enjoyment of sex is noble, not base. All human desires can be transformed into enlightenment.

The sound A *represents the Womb Realm, Mother, Great Compassion, and the Red Lotus. The sound* UN *represents the Diamond Realm, Father, Great Wisdom, and the White Stupa.* A/UN *is Female/Male, Yin/Yang, Ocean/Mountain, Mercy/Charity, Emptiness/Form. The red seed from the female and the white seed from the male bring human beings into existence. The unity and integration of* A/UN *creates and sustains the universe. This is the truth, not falsehood.*

Prior to performing these rites, the man and woman take these vows:

1. *We trust in the teachings of the Tachikawa Ryu.*
2. *We vow to cooperate and come together in mutual accord in body and mind at all times.*
3. *We vow to perform these rites carefully under strict supervision by a master.*
4. *We vow not to argue or fight.*
5. *We vow not to compete, criticize, or blame each other.*
6. *We vow not to overeat or overdrink.*

The Buddha couple should bathe together in a curative hot spring without physical contact. The couple must be in perfect accord in body, mind, and speech. The couple must be in a bright, positive mood, free of gloom, despair, or unhappiness. The man is to be venerated as Fudo Myo-o; the woman embodies Aizen Myo-o. (The esoteric meaning of "Fudo Myo-o" is "man and woman in unbreakable union"; "Aizen Myo-o" is "man and woman irrevocably stained with passion.") The holy couple faces each other and they make three prostrations, reciting, "I aspire to enter the womb realm" in the case of the man, and "I aspire to receive the diamond realm" in the case of the woman.

The room must be spotlessly clean, well hidden, with a small altar. The secret Buddha image is kept veiled, not to be uncovered until after the rites have been performed. (The instructions regarding the Buddha image can only be imparted orally and are never to be written down.) Fresh flowers are placed on the altar, together with appropriate seasonal offerings from the mountains and the sea. Kindle fragrant incense. Light the room with five candles.

The best Buddha image is one's own body. Therefore, the man and the woman shed their robes in the corner and face each other completely naked and unadorned. Midnight is the ideal time to begin the rites. The man crosses his legs in the meditation posture and the woman sits on top of the man and lets his jewel enter her lotus. During the sexual congress of the two roots of existence, the breath should be harmonized in an A *(in) and* UN *(out) rhythm. The man should keep his jewel*

*pressed against the woman's womb as they meditate together,
blending the male/female components of the five elements:
earth, water, fire, air, and space. If done properly, this blending of the elements will form a five-colored rainbow: yellow,
blue, red, green, and white. The mother/father Buddha posture is best, but other postures and magic chants are allowed.
(Secret instruction.)*

*However, at the break of dawn when the rooster crows,
the Buddha couple should be in the mother/father posture. At
that time, the Buddha couple should come to a mutual instant
of bliss; that is the moment of truth, a state of pure ecstasy, an
unobstructed integration of emptiness and form. This is the
realm of Dainichi, the cosmic Buddha where myriad elements
exist in perfect equilibrium. All hail!*

After Dai-en had made a copy of this astonishing text,
he brought the original back to Kakusho.

"In order to understand the secret Tachikawa Ryu
teachings," Kakusho began, "you need actual practice, not
just the theory contained in this text. I will introduce you
to a female flesh-and-blood partner, a *dakini*. She will be
your master. Before I introduce you to her, however, you
need to make a vow of the ultimate sacrifice. If you fail to
complete the training or violate the rules of training, you
will take your own life. Agreed?"

Dai-en understood that such a suicide vow was made
for the most serious forms of training in his school—it was
do or die. He immediately went to the main hall, pros-

trated himself before the Great Sun Buddha, and made the solemn vow to sacrifice his life by leaping off the top of a huge waterfall if he did not complete the training.

When Dai-en returned to the abbot's quarters, Kakusho said, "Prepare for a pilgrimage. You will be gone at least several months, and you may never return. I will write a letter of introduction while you are getting ready for your journey."

Dai-en had few possessions, so he was ready to go in a short time.

"About three hours walk from here, there is a mountain shrine called Wago Jinja. I have drawn a map—destroy it when you arrive. Ask the shrine couple there to bring you to Gessho, the nun 'Moon Beam.' She lives in a hermitage adjacent to the shrine. Give her this letter of introduction, and a donation of all the money you have."

Dai-en was on his way. He walked quickly, and in a couple of hours he was on the outskirts of the city. He found the mountain path with some difficulty: it was very narrow, and the forest was thick. Suddenly, though, he came to a little, very well kept village. The shrine gate was clearly visible, and he proceeded up the stone stairs.

An older couple was out in front of the shrine. Couples married for a long time often begin to look alike, but this man and woman looked extraordinarily similar—the same size, wearing pure white robes and long, flowing grey hair. Both had clear, wrinkle-free complexions. They were a perfect match.

Stone Dosojin image: Day (top) and Night (bottom).

Stone Dosojin statue: a perfect match.

"I am the Shingon monk Dai-en from Kongo-ji," he announced.

"We know," the couple said in unison. "We have been waiting for you. We will take you to Gessho."

Since Dai-en had left the temple almost immediately, he wondered how news of his visit had arrived before him.

Dai-en noticed that the shrine was small but neat, and that there were many Dosojin (stone images of a male and female couple) on the grounds. Such sex-god statues were common in the countryside, though, and there was nothing remarkable about their presence here.

The hermitage, which was down a bit from the shrine, had the look of a small Buddhist temple. There was a waterfall not far away, a little vegetable garden, a rock garden, and some fruit trees.

The nun Gessho was standing out in front of the hermitage.

"Come in," she beckoned. "I have been expecting you." She was of indeterminate age, tiny, with sharp features and very bright eyes. She appeared robust and her movements were agile. Her head was shaved, and she was wearing dark monastic work clothes.

The inside of her hermitage was fragrant, but the incense smell was much different from that of a normal temple. (Dai-en later learned that the incense was a potent mixture of aloeswood, cloves, sandalwood, rosemary, and an exotic perfume of flowers imported from abroad.) After the formal greetings, Dai-en handed Gessho the letter of introduction.

"I know what it says," she said matter-of-factly. "You seem sincere. I will give you instruction in the Tachikawa Ryu teachings under these conditions: You will follow my instructions at all times, you will not leave without my full consent, and you will keep a vow of complete secrecy."

"I vow to accept all those conditions," Dai-en proclaimed.

Gessho continued, "The aim of the Tachikawa Ryu is supreme awakening. This is the greatest of challenges. You must be willing to risk your life, and that is why we made you take a suicide vow. There have been those who have claimed that mere sexual intercourse will make you a Buddha. Those people are heretics. There are no teachings more profound or more difficult to master than those of the Tachikawa Ryu."

"I understand," said Daien.

"We will sleep in the same room but there will be no physical contact until I say so. Store your belongings on this shelf. There is a hot spring bath in the back. After you bathe, you will sleep here," she pointed to a space in the next room. "Get some rest. Change into these clothes tomorrow."

The training commenced the next day at dawn. Gessho was serious and focused, but not strident or fanatical. After their morning toilet, Gessho told Dai-en, "Every morning will begin with 108 prostrations, not to a Buddha image of stone or wood, but to the image of Buddha within us." Thus, Gessho and Dai-en faced each other and started the prostrations. Dai-en followed Gessho's lead, and the pace was steady. He now realized why Gessho was in such good condition.

After the prostrations were complete, Gessho led Dai-en outside and down the path to the waterfall. The natural waterfall was a torrent, but a man-made waterfall had been constructed near it. Two steady streams poured down from the artificial wall, and there was a stone basin underneath where two people could stand safely. Dai-en had done *misogi* (ritual purification) in a waterfall previously, and he knew what to do. He stripped down to his loincloth, performed the preparatory rites, and stepped into the first waterfall. While he was chanting in the ritual posture, Gessho, wearing a short white robe, stepped in the falls next to him. The waterfall purification rite took about thirty minutes.

After changing into dry clothes, Gessho announced, "We will now eat at the shrine. We do so twice a day."

The shrine couple had prepared the food for the four of them. It was mountain fare: wild vegetables, nuts, pickled daikon, dried fruit, roots, a hearty bowl of thick miso soup, a small bowl of rice mixed with barley, and wild boar meat. Dai-en was surprised by the last item since Buddhists were usually vegetarian, especially during training.

"For your stamina," said Gessho, who had read Dai-en's mind.

After breakfast, the pair returned to the hermitage.

"We will conduct the secret Shoten rite every morning at this time," Gessho declared.

"This is the story of Shoten," Gessho began. "There was an elephant-headed god called Binayaka. He was gang-leader of a bunch of mischief-making demons that created all kinds of trouble for people. In order to control Binayaka and his minions, Kannon, the Goddess of Compassion, incarnated herself as a beautiful woman. As soon as he set eyes on her, Binayaka lusted for her. 'I will submit to your advances,' she told him, 'if you promise to mend your evil ways and follow Buddha. From now on, you will be a "Remover of Obstacles," not a "Creator of Obstacles."' Binayaka was so smitten with the beautiful woman that he agreed. They embraced.

"Their embrace is represented by the image called Shoten. They both have elephant heads, and they are fused together as one in a state of peaceful rejoicing. Notice that in this image the female is standing on the male's feet to control him—just in case he tries to revert to his old untamed nature," Gessho explained.

"We will anoint the image 108 times with sesame oil as we chant a mantra," Gessho continued. "We ask for the Shoten couple's guidance to enable us to eradicate the obstacles of greed, pride, and vanity in our minds and to transform our raging passions into the repose of enlightenment. The male Shoten is Dainichi, and the female Shoten is Kannon."

Tachikawa Ryu Shoten couple.

The Shoten altar held the following items: flowers (representing the sense of sight); a bell (sound); red cloth (touch); an incense burner (smell); and fruit, cakes, and rice wine (taste). In the center of the altar was the mother/father Shoten image in the middle of a bowl.

Dai-en noticed that placed on a separate shelf was a lovely wooden image of Naked Benten, the goddess of love, learning, music, and art.

"She is my personal guardian deity," Gessho said. "I carved the image myself."

"After the Shoten rite, we will partake of the offerings on the altar—sweets, fruits, and sips of rice wine," Gessho said. (Dai-en was amazed at the wonderful taste of the womb-shaped sweets. Called "bliss cakes," they were made from a secret recipe, and they were delicious.)

"And then there will be *ajikan* meditation," Gessho told Dai-en.

Dai-en had done *ajikan* meditation often but, as he discovered, the Tachikawa Ryu version was very different.

"In regular *ajikan* mediation," Gessho said, "the practitioner sits before a painting of the cosmic seed-syllable A set within a circle representing the full moon and employs various visualizations. However, here is the *ajikan* image we use in the Tachikawa Ryu."

Gessho unveiled the mandala painting: the seed-syllable A was placed over the genitals of a man and woman lying flat and in sexual congress.

"Eventually you need to practice with a flesh-and-

Naked Benzaiten, the goddess of love, learning, music, and art.

blood partner," Gessho explained. "But first you must identify with the male and female elements within yourself. Initially, you visualize yourself as the male in the mandala, which should not be hard given your present incarnation, but then you also must visualize yourself as the female in the mandala. In the Tachikawa Ryu we in fact believe that every man has been a woman in a previous existence and vice versa. You need to join the red and white currents, the male and female consciousness, in your heart. I will guide your meditation for the first week or so."

After the meditation was completed Gessho told Dai-en what their daily schedule would be.

"From now until the fourth hour of the afternoon is free time. Each day, I will give you some chores to do, but you will also have time to memorize the texts, chants, and ritual gestures, and perhaps rest a bit. We will eat again at the fourth hour. Following the meal and a short break, the mother/father Buddha activity training will commence."

The second and last meal of the day was less substantial than the first, but Dai-en still was satisfied. The food was much tastier and more abundant than the meals he was accustomed to in the monastery. Dai-en felt well nourished.

Gessho gave Dai-en some texts to study. The words meant little to him, like those of most secret texts; the inner meaning had to be imparted by the *ajari* (master), which was what Gessho did later. Here is an excerpt from one of them, *The One Mind Sutra:*

In the beginning was the Void. All things were One. There was no start, no end. Within the Void, a light emerged, the Great Sun, then the two drops and five elements activated. This is the source of life.

In Shinto, the primordial life force is known as Kunitokotachi no mikoto; in Daoism, it is known as the Great Ultimate; in Tendai, it is known as Original Awakening; in Shingon, it is known as Dainichi, the Sun Buddha; in Jodo, it is known as Amida's Original Vow; in Zen, it is known as Buddha-nature; in Astrology it is known as Ancient of Days.

In order for a body to appear, there must be a spirit to animate it. In most places this spirit is called "god." This spirit always has a male and female aspect; the interaction between the male and female spirit gave birth to existence.

When Gotama became Buddha, after he had taken a nourishing meal and had sex with the milkmaid Sujata, his enlightenment revealed to him the true nature of the universe: All existence manifests the interaction of the sun (male) and moon (female), or as we call it, the white and red drops. Shintoists, Daoists, and Confucians also believe that the mingling of these two elements brought the world into being.

One element is light, like air, and is manifest in wood and fire; it is the male principle we call Sunlight Bodhisattva. The complementary element is heavy, like earth, and manifest in metal and water. It is the female principle we call Moonlight Bodhisattva. We also use the terms Diamond Realm and Womb Realm.

The interaction of those two Realms when a man and woman unite forms the purest elixir from which life springs. Sexual congress is the supreme Buddha activity.

It was time for instruction. Gessho lit the room with candles and kindled fragrant incense.

"We will always begin the mother/father Buddha activity training with a brief fire ceremony," Gessho began. "This is not the external fire ceremony to which you are accustomed. Instead of tossing hundreds of prayer sticks into a raging fire in a cauldron while reciting prayers, in the Tachikawa Ryu the fire ceremony is internal. The fire of one's passion is to be transmuted into the gold of enlightenment. Set your passions ablaze and consume your negative thoughts: delusion, selfishness, attachment, insensitivity, pride, arrogance, hostility, confusion, envy, and greed. Your status and role, your name and form, must be burnt to ashes."

The Buddha activity training had begun. The training was methodical and thorough. It had to be. In his entire life, Dai-en had sexual contact with only two women—the courtesan Goddess of Compassion and Lady Hotoke. He needed to learn everything about a woman. The first weeks of instruction focused on knowledge and use of the body, which in Tachikawa Ryu teachings is the body of a Buddha. Gessho told him that the body was a miniature universe. She read this text to him:

All Buddhas are part of the same body. All sentient beings are contained in the Buddha body as well. All sentient beings have the capacity for enlightenment but do not realize this fact. They know nothing of skillful means. They are sunk in the ocean of birth and death. They are lost in ignorance and cannot scale the peak of enlightenment. However, if good men and good women learn the proper gestures with their hands, the proper chants with their mouths, and keep the quest to become Buddha in this very body in their minds, they can become one with Dainichi in body, speech, and mind. A true couple will become Buddha!

Gessho patiently and in detail showed Dai-en how different sections of his body reacted to various stimuli—tactile and aural.

"You must develop a body that is sensitive to various kinds of touch and sounds. Every nerve, joint, and muscle must be energized." Gessho explained the different nerve lines along the left and right sides of the body and described how they should meet in the center. During this part of the training, she gently touched Dai-en all over his body—forehead, eyes, nostrils, mouth, arms, torso, thighs, legs, the bottom of his feet—with her left hand while she recited various mantra (secret chants) and performed mudra (ritual gestures) with her right hand. Gessho gave him instructions on how to massage his little buddha and told him which exercises and pressure points were effective for generating sexual energy. She eventually began to caress

Dai-en's little buddha and his golden sack (testicles) in a most reverent manner.

This instruction went on for some time. Dai-en was rather intimidated at first, and he was trying hard to remember all the mantras and mudras. So he was able to prevent himself from trying to have intercourse with Gessho.

Then it was Dai-en's turn to venerate Gessho's body. Gessho unrobed completely, and for the first time Dai-en saw her naked. She was tiny but with nicely shaped breasts with nipples like stars, and she had a well-proportioned, supple body. Gessho's jade gate was lovely and prominent. (She called it her *oku-no-in,* "inner temple of truth.") Her skin was radiant and wonderful to touch. Her fingernails were lustrous like mother-of-pearl. Again the instructions for venerating the body were long and involved, longer than those required for a man because much attention needed to be spent on massaging, licking, and sucking the breasts and on how to handle the very sensitive, and different, parts of a woman's lotus. There was a special *kuji-giri,* "nine-cut pattern," for moving the fingers within a female partner's lotus.

Gessho taught Dai-en how to develop acute sensitivity to a lover: "View your lover's embrace as the best touch; view your lover's kiss as the best taste; view your lover's breath as the best fragrance; view your lover's sighs as the best sound; view the ecstasy in your lover's eyes as the best sight; and view being as one with your lover as the best thought."

The entire process of learning about the body took months, and then they started the practice of embracing. There were twelve different kinds of embrace in the Tachikawa Ryu—variations of face-to-face, side-to-side, even back-to-back—and Gessho insisted that they spend at least thirty minutes a time in a given posture.

Kissing was the next stage. It was a total mystery to Dai-en. He had been raised by monks and had never seen a couple kiss. In those days people never kissed in public. Even in private, kissing was rare, considered an act so intimate and erotic that it was best left to the denizens of the pleasure quarters. The skillful movements of Gessho's lips and tongue were jolting—a few times, Dai-en almost lost consciousness.

Dai-en received and learned how to apply a "tongue bath." "Saliva—we call it 'diamond lacquer'—removes all the poisons from the skin and turns them into nectar," Gessho assured him. "As you know," she continued, "Unity of body, mind, and speech is the goal of Shingon training. So the mouth and what it produces is very important. The mouth can utter the worst blasphemies or sing the sweetest songs. In the Tachikawa Ryu, union of the lips between the partners is a prime method of circulating energy."

Finally, it was time to enact the supreme rite. Gessho said to Dai-en, "When we come together, you will likely not be able to contain yourself. It is permitted to release your shower of baby buddhas (sperm) inside my lotus—I am past the age where I can conceive—but try to hold out as long as you can." (Dai-en was surprised by the statement that Gessho was of the age where she could not longer conceive—he had thought she was in her mid-thirties.)

As Gessho expected, Dai-en was largely hopeless the first few weeks of their mother/father Buddha training. He had done an admirable job of containing himself through the long preliminaries, but once inside Gessho's treasure of treasures—her lotus was tight, sweet-smelling, and very moist—he was gone almost immediately.

Over the following months, Dai-en got much more skillful, even mastering the art of achieving bliss without ejaculating. (He still preferred the bliss of total release, however. And Gessho had told him, "Unlike the Daoist sex magicians who believe that every ejaculation shortens a man's life, in the Tachikawa Ryu we prefer generous and copious emission of sexual fluids for both man and woman—the more love juice, the better.") There were forty-eight postures of love in the Tachikawa Ryu. Some were very strenuous—and ingenious, Dai-en often thought—and the accompanying mantras and mudras were mind-boggling. Gessho insisted that they try them all but later admitted that the "Lady Buddha on Top" posture—the Tachikawa Ryu had nine variations—was the one that afforded most females the best chance of achieving bliss. ("That is why some men are afraid of letting women get on top," Gessho mentioned once. "They are afraid of letting women have control even in sex.")

Breath control was very important during love-making, Gessho told Dai-en. There were these levels of mother/ father Buddha activity: desire, contact, congress, fulfillment, and enlightenment. She elaborated: "In more concrete terms, these levels are expressed in the acts of smiling at each other, holding hands, gazing into each others' eyes, embracing and kissing, and sexual union. Progress through each level must be gradual and each level experienced fully." The ideal for the couple was to always be centered in each other—the "Middle Way" that Buddha proclaimed—and ride the waves of ecstasy together to the end.

"There are different levels of pleasure between a man and woman," Gessho explained further. "The lowest is physical pleasure. Most couples remain stuck at that level. In the Tachikawa Ryu, however, we want to progress from the physical to the mental, and then on to the spiritual."

Later, Gessho explained the progression from initial impulse to supreme enlightenment in more detail. "In the Tachikawa Ryu," she said, "we posit seventeen stages in the path:

1. *The innate attraction to the opposite sex that all beings possess, which we call mother/father Buddha-nature.*
2. *Kindling of desire*
3. *Physical contact*
4. *Embrace*
5. *Mutual affection*
6. *Perception of the beauty of one's partner*

7. *Joy of intercourse*
8. *Love*
9. *Satisfaction (orgasm)*
10. *Adornment of the body and mind*
11. *Bliss*
12. *Radiance*
13. *Ecstasy*
14. *Delight in physical forms*
15. *Faultless speech*
16. *Pure fragrance (enjoyment of all life)*
17. *Pure taste (total fulfillment)"*

Dai-en was confused about some of this—especially about the subtle differences between "satisfaction," "bliss," "ecstasy," and "total fulfillment."

"We all are," Gessho assured him. "In the Tachikawa Ryu we speak of four levels of bliss: natural, spiritual, nondual, and cosmic. The levels are derived from actual experiences. I have given them to you as reference points, to guide you as your practice widens and your experience deepens. They can never be adequately explained in words."

Following the mother/father Buddha training, they had a short session of "insight mediation," which is meditation without visualization, with the eyes half open. One settles down in an attempt to see things as they really are—in this case, to appreciate the reality of the mother/father Buddha activity. Before retiring, Gessho and Dai-en shared a small cup of a medicinal drink made with rice wine and herbs. (Gessho later showed Dai-en how to concoct the brew. She also gave him lessons in preparing various aphrodisiac medicines—including one that was made of ingredients the Medicine Buddha had taught a famous priest in a dream, and another called "Bliss Bestowing Pills for Ladies.")

From the beginning of the training, Gessho and Dai-en took one day off a week to walk the "mountain mandala," as Gessho called it, in the forest that surrounded them. The circular course through the mountain took four to five hours to complete. Along the way, they stopped and offered appropriate prayers at small shrines, stone Buddha and Dosojin images, sacred rocks and trees, and hidden caves.

One day, after they had been doing the mountain pilgrimage for some weeks, Gessho surprised Dai-en by suddenly removing the bottom of her work kimono and instructing him to put his little buddha in her lotus, right then! Thereafter, such impromptu mother/father Buddha activity became a regular part of the course and was Dai-en's favorite part of the training. Indoors, Gessho's instruction was methodical but, outdoors, she was more spontaneous, and Dai-en sensed that she let herself go more. They walked all through the year, even when there was much snow; the winter walks were shorter, but Dai-en found them bracing (and erotic). At the peak of the mountain, they took a ten-minute sunbathe in the nude.

During one of these mountain walks, Gessho told Dai-en how important it is to experience the power of nature.

"Creation begins with sex," she said. "Sexual energy is what we need to harness and transform. It is the force that activates this world of ours. The entire cosmos is one huge sex organ with male and female components fused together!"

There were short periods of abstinence lasting from three to nine days, in which they would have no physical contact. There were also regular one-day fasts to "purge the body of poisons," as Gessho put it. Dai-en felt that the periodic resting and fasting really helped—he never felt better and was in radiant good health.

Dai-en eventually discovered what the secret image was on the altar. It was a skull. After engaging in the mother/father Buddha activity, Gessho would carefully collect their sexual effluvia and rub it on the skull. ("She was one of the Matriarchs of the Tachikawa Ryu," Gessho matter-of-factly informed Dai-en when he first saw the skull.) "Remember, we are Buddhists," Gessho told him, "and the first principle of Buddhism is that all things are impermanent. We are born to die. To accept that reality is an essential teaching of the Tachikawa Ryu."

Gessho was very careful about gathering all their sexual effluvia. She considered it a sacred substance, and she told Dai-en that one Tachikawa Ryu temple had a yearly memorial service for all the "unused" sperm that was sacrificed by couples during sex in the preceding twelve months.

When Dai-en had been with Gessho for almost a thousand days, Gessho told him that his training with her would be finished soon. They would refrain from all contact for nine days and then perform the rite described in the text that Dai-en had first received from Kakusho.

In addition to suggestions for birth control, Gessho gave Dai-en some final practical advice: "Avoid making love in storms, when in mourning, or when you or your partner is in mental or physical distress." She also had him copy a very interesting text on Tachikawa Ryu embryology:

In the Tachikawa Ryu couples are not afraid to have children when the conditions are right; that is part of life, and we see every offspring as a child of Buddha. The best kind of mother/father Buddha activity often results in a child being conceived. We believe that a different Buddha watches over a fetus each month of his or her development. Keep this text for future reference.

Dai-en once asked Gessho about the village. Although there were ten or so houses there, he saw only older couples, no children. In the warmer months, each couple had two to six boarders, presumably trainees.

"Yes," Gessho explained. "All the people living here are older couples (except for me). And they are all associated with the Tachikawa Ryu. Most of the couples have been together for ages, and they no longer need to toil full-time in the world below. This is where they come to teach and spend their final years. It is very cold and snowy here, but we have a hot spring that provides warmth during the long winter.

"The Tachikawa Ryu has many different aspects," Gessho continued. "The shrine couple follows essentially Daoist teachings, attempting to attain immortality through sex magic. Another couple, nominal adherents of the Nichiren School, function as soothsayers. We also have a *yamabushi* (mountain wizard) pair who act as healers. One couple are sorcerers who specialize in casting spells and black magic. They do the work with the skulls and horse penises." (Dai-en knew which couple that was—they were the only ones who made him ill at ease when he saw them.)

"In the future," Gessho added, "you may want to train with some of them, but that is up to you. For example, I have not taught you the Skull and Horse Penis Rituals because they are not what I am most interested in personally, but you may want to look into them. Also, in some branches of the Tachikawa Ryu, couplings are more random and frequent. You may want to experience that type of training. We find, however, that stable, long-term relationships are most conducive for deep and sustained training.

"My partner," Gessho said, again reading Dai-en's mind, "entered nirvana while we were performing one of the Tachikawa Ryu rites a few years ago. His name was Nissho, 'Sun Beam.'"

Dai-en had also noticed highly unusual posthumous Buddhist names engraved on the tombstones in the small cemetery: Sister Secret Flower Divine Bud, Sister Bottomless Cavern of Bliss, Sister Seed of All Pleasure, Nun Crimson Moon Wondrous Space, Brother Direct Entry into Buddhahood, Brother Skillful Granter of Grace, Monk Forever in the Saddle, and the like. "Yes," Gessho told him, "those are all names that identify people as outstanding members of the Tachikawa Ryu."

"I have initiated you into the techniques of the Tachikawa Ryu," Gessho said one day, "but you lack one element for true understanding: heartfelt love for your partner. I have been a vehicle for you to practice with. That is fine—that is my function, which I accept and enjoy. However, much of our training has been mechanical, and you need real passion for a partner to attain Buddha bliss in this very body. That passion has to be spontaneous and reciprocated. And that feeling even transcends sex. Sexual congress is the result of love, not the cause. Your partner may know nothing about the Tachikawa Ryu, but it is still possible to attain the ultimate together if you apply the skillful means that I have taught you. It is time for you to return to the world, and search for a true partner.

"Never forget the essential teaching of the Tachikawa Ryu," Gessho commanded. "Equality. Equality between the male and female on all levels—cosmic, social, individual, and sexual. True equality results in equanimity, the equanimity that Buddha instructed us to strive for. Your

Mother/Father Buddha couple: One harmonious whole, this joyful and peaceful couple is serene and strong in their togetherness. Their union represents the resolution of all dichotomies and antagonisms.

ultimate partner will be on the same level and plane of development."

It was true, Dai-en realized, that even though he and Gessho had been intimate physically in every possible manner, there was a reserve between them. Gessho was his master. While they would never be true equals as partners, Dai-en hoped that some day he would equal Gessho in spirit.

The final mother/father Buddha activity ceremony was sublime. Dai-en parted company with Gessho the next day. He made one full prostration a minute in length, got up, and left the village.

Dai-en returned to Kongo-ji, not knowing what to expect. Kakusho was not surprised by his appearance. He told him, "Make the pilgrimage to the eighty-eight temples in Shikoku. The weather is warmer there, and the pilgrimage will keep you occupied for at least a few months. People are kind there, and you can survive as a mendicant monk. You will have a different set of experiences that will further deepen your understanding."

HOTOKE WAS NOT embarrassed by her encounter with the monk Dai-en—it did not leave her pregnant fortunately—

but she was surprised she was so aroused. Even though her occupation in the pleasure quarters was to sleep with many different men, courtesans were counseled from the start of their careers never to let their passions get out of control. A courtesan should always act as a role-player in sex, and never as an active participant in a love affair. To give one's heart to a man, even a patron as noble as Hidemune, was

Tachikawa Ryu Monastic Worship.

believed to be a sure recipe for disaster. Although Hotoke had real affection for Hidemune, she would not describe her feelings as "love."

After her fling with the monk Dai-en, though, Hotoke felt restless. She was vaguely troubled, not at ease. She had been fortunate as a courtesan and concubine, leading a largely sheltered life, and her physical circumstances were good, but she was no longer satisfied with her existence.

In the past, on many mornings when Hotoke awoke, she found Hidemune sitting in meditation in the adjacent room. When she asked him what he was doing, he said, "*Zazen.* I try to sit every morning. I learned how to meditate from Abbot Dosen." At the time, Hotoke did not pursue the matter—she was not interested. Lately, however, she wondered what Hidemune had gotten from his meditation. She had heard some of the other courtesans talk about the abbot Dosen—"He is not like most men—he is kind and considerate to women like us."

Hotoke decided to visit Dosen.

Although Dosen was supposed to be living in seclusion, having passed on the abbot's position of Tokai-ji to one of his disciples, his hermitage was always full of people—lords, samurai, monks, nuns, pleasure girls, entertainers, artists, merchants, craftsmen, coolies, beggars. When Hotoke was finally given an audience, Dosen replied to her introduction, "Yes, Lady Hotoke. Lord Hidemune often mentioned you."

Dosen was older, probably in his upper seventies, but he had a friendly, slightly impish smile.

"What do you need?" Dosen asked Hotoke.

"I don't know exactly," Hotoke confessed. "Can you teach me Zen meditation?"

"If you really want to learn, I will teach you," Dosen said unceremoniously. "Since you are so pretty, the monks will pester you, but I have a small, separate group of ladies—some may be your former companions, in fact—that sit every morning at six. See you tomorrow?"

Hotoke came to the temple the following morning at 5:30 a.m.

"The ladies here all sit in *seiza*, on their knees, rather than in *zazen*, the formal meditation posture," Dosen said. "That is fine. At the beginning, just focus on counting your breathing, one count for each inhalation/exhalation, up to ten, and then start again. Keep your eyes half open, softly fixed on a spot about a meter in front of you."

Although this seemed to be the easiest thing in the world to do—simply breathe—Hotoke discovered that she was easily distracted by random thoughts and that she frequently lost count of her breaths.

"Don't worry," Dosen counseled Hotoke. "Continue to sit every day, and your concentration will get better."

Hotoke did indeed become more proficient at sitting still, but Dosen had a surprise for her: "I want you to tell me where you were before your parents were born. You have to give me an answer each week."

Stone Dosojin statue with the couple dressed as a monk and a nun.

Hotoke was speechless for the first few interviews. She had never considered such questions before. Nevertheless, she did not give up, and she gamely began to offer some answers—"In space?" "Over there?"—all of which were immediately rejected by Dosen.

Much to her surprise, Hotoke felt tremendously aroused during meditation even though she was sitting with a bunch of women in a non-stimulating, quiet atmosphere. She found Zen meditation to be extremely erotic.

Hotoke confessed this fact to Dosen. "Yes, I understand," he said in sympathy. Some of the ladies want to become nuns, and I allow a few of the older ones to do so. But for young women like you, I believe it better to have a partner to help you understand the sexual dimension of life. The puzzle I have given you—Where were you before your parents were born?—is also part of that dimension."

Hotoke was stunned to hear this coming from a Buddhist monk.

"Have you heard of the Tachikawa Ryu?" Dosen asked.

Once Hotoke had heard some of the courtesans talking about the Tachikawa Ryu, but she did not know what it was.

"It was a school of Buddhism that taught that sex is the way to enlightenment. Most people considered it a Shingon sect, but in fact there is a lot of Zen in the teachings. One of the patriarchs of the Tachikawa Ryu, who was called Monkan, composed this Zen verse:

Willows are green,
Flowers are red.
Things just as they are
Constitute Buddha-nature;
The natural coupling of male and female
Is Buddhahood!

"You have heard of Ikkyu?"

"Yes, of course," Hotoke replied. "Everyone knows about Ikkyu."

"Do you know the story of the treasure house of Buddhism?" Dosen asked.

Hotoke shook her head no.

"One day Ikkyu was traveling in an isolated district when he happened to see a naked woman bathing in a river. Ikkyu stopped and reverently bowed three times in the direction of her jade gate. A passerby who had witnessed the scene asked Ikkyu to explain his behavior as a Buddhist monk: 'Why did you bow to that foul sex organ?'

"Ikkyu replied sharply, 'Women are the treasure house of Buddhism. They are the source out of which every being came forth, including Buddha and Bodhidharma!'

"Bodhidharma is the founder of the Zen school," Dosen continued. "One teaching attributed to him is *Kensho Jobutsu*, 'See into your nature, and become Buddha.' It can also be interpreted as meaning, 'See into the nature of sex, and that will make you a Buddha,' the same teaching as the Tachikawa Ryu. Have you read any of Ikkyu's poetry?"

Hotoke had not.

"I will give you a copy of his poems to read. You will enjoy them. Here is a poem of mine for you to think about:

Falling in love is dangerous,
For passion is the source of illusion;
Yet being in love gives life flavor,
And passions themselves
Can bring one to enlightenment.

These are a few of Ikkyu's poems that Hotoke later read:

The lotus flower
Is not stained by the mud;
This dewdrop form,
Alone, just as it is,
Manifests the real body of truth.

Crimson cheeks, light colored hair, full of compassion
*   and love.*
Lost in a dream of love-play, I contemplate her
*   beauty.*
One thousand eyes of Great Mercy look upon
all but see no one beyond redemption.
This Goddess is found in every woman.

Hidden by a river or sea, in the mountains,
A man of the Way shuns fame and fortune.
Night after night, we two love birds
snuggle on the meditation platform,
Lost in dalliance, intimate talk, and orgasmic
  bliss.

Although Hotoke was confused by Dosen's talks, he assured her that "confusion and doubt were good for Zen training."

"One needs to really deal with the ultimate problems of life, in actual situations," Dosen told Hotoke. "The answers will come eventually. Just continue sitting in meditation each morning, and see me for an interview once a week."

Hotoke did so assiduously. For three years.

DAI-EN HAD BEGUN his pilgrimage on Mount Koya, headquarters of his Shingon School of Buddhism. The founder of the Shingon School, Kukai—Kobo Daishi—was believed still to be in meditation on the mountain. Dai-en visited the temple where Kobo Daishi was said to be sitting and silently prayed to the Shingon patriarch for guidance.

From Koya, which is on a mountain in central Japan on the main island of Honshu, Dai-en made his way down to the southern island of Shikoku, beginning a circuit. It takes at least two months to walk the eighty-eight-temple circuit and visit other important places along the route. Dai-en was in no hurry, however. And, since he was a Shingon priest and most of the temples were associated with the Shingon School, he was often asked by the local abbots to stay on and help out with the temple work for a while. Dai-en usually agreed to do so. In fact, he lingered at the last temple, Okubo-ji, number eighty-eight, for several months.

The abbot of Okubo-ji was learned and experienced. He taught Dai-en the Shingon "Morning Star Meditation," the meditation practice that was said to have given Kukai his initial glimpse of enlightenment. The meditation was performed in a cave at night.

One day, the abbot told Dai-en that there was to be a "Sex Emancipation Day" in the area soon.

"As you have noticed, life is hard in the mountains," the abbot said. "People are not lazy here, but they really have to toil to get enough food to last the whole year, and they don't have any time to play. As in many rural districts, the local lord decided to establish a Sex Emancipation Day festival once a year to let people blow off steam and add spice to their lives. In midsummer the entire village gathers in the early afternoon to dance, drink, and eat. By nightfall everyone is in a festive mood, and people begin to pair up. It is the custom for each man and woman to have sex with at least three different people before sunrise the next morning.

"You should join this year," the abbot told Dai-en. "You will enjoy it. Kobo Daishi taught that we must have enlightenment in this very *body*, not just our *mind*. It will be a good experience for you—you will learn more about the normal feelings of human beings."

"Won't the villagers be upset if a monk joins the Festival?" Dai-en asked. "Normally you are expected to behave appropriately for a monk," the abbot replied. "But this really is a Sex Emancipation Day—everyone is given a dispensation. Even me," he said smiling.

Haru, a local farmer's wife, was looking forward to participating in the festival. She enjoyed sex. Like most of the girls in the village, she had got her husband through *yo-bai* ("night prowling"). In *yo-bai*, a young man wrapped his face with a cloth and stealthily entered a young woman's bedroom at night. Although a pretense was made that the nighttime visit was sudden and unexpected, most young girls had given a sign that such a visit would be welcomed beforehand. The parents also were in on the charade—they conveniently left the door open and made sure that their daughter was sleeping alone.

Haru liked *yo-bai* from the start. Yosuke, the man she had ended up with, was actually the fourth *yo-bai* she had entertained. He was the one who had gotten her pregnant. Yosuke was not a bad fellow, but Haru worked from dawn to dusk on the farm, and she cared for her husband, children, and aged parents. Yosuke enjoyed the Festival, too, but Haru felt that he liked the drinking and camaraderie with other farmers more than the free sex. Although they never talked about what had transpired that day—that was taboo—Haru felt that Yosuke had sex with only one or two women, more out of obligation than actual relish. Haru, on the other hand, always had intercourse with at least three men, sometimes five or six.

In *yo-bai*, a girl pretty much knew who was coming, but, in the Festival, things were more random. Haru liked this aspect, even though everyone had favorites with whom they wanted to connect. Getting pregnant was a possibility, of course, but being with child was the lot of women in those days—and, of the four children whom Haru had borne, the two that survived infancy were children conceived during the Festival.

On the day of the Festival, Dai-en dressed in a light peasant kimono. The abbot saw him off. Although he had suggested to Dai-en that he would be an active participant, the abbot had in fact not joined the Festival since he had become chief priest years before.

The weather was good. It was a sultry summer day during the brief lull between the arduous labors of planting and harvesting. There was more drinking than eating, and there was much energetic dancing in big circles.

Haru had her eye on Dai-en. He was a newcomer, and he looked strong and fresh. As soon as it got dark, Haru grabbed Dai-en by the sleeve and led him off. She knew exactly where to go—a little patch of ground down the hill a bit behind the shrine. Haru was frantic, and Dai-en had no chance to use his Tachikawa Ryu love-making skills. She pulled him down on top of her. She sighed deeply when he entered her jade gate, and her toes curled with bliss after a minute or two of thrusting. Haru held Dai-en very tightly for some time.

"Thank you," Haru found herself saying, which was not usual during the Festival. In a few moments, she recovered, sprang up, and sped back to the dancing.

"I am in a hurry," she said laughing.

Dai-en was touched by her passion. It was earthy and uncomplicated. It was sex, pure and simple, seemingly with none of the philosophical underpinnings involved in Tachikawa Ryu love-making. Nevertheless, Dai-en felt that there had been something present in their embracing that was deeper than just unbridled lust. (He was not sure what Haru felt.)

To tell the truth, Dai-en was finished for the night. He had no desire to dally with someone else. He passed a few couples who were gaily laughing on the way back to the temple.

"There is another sex festival in January," the abbot told Dai-en the next day. "I don't know if you realized it, but Okubo-ji can be taken to mean 'Great Pussy Temple.' We have a Horny Goddess of Compassion and a Randy Buddha of Healing enshrined here, and people come from all over to pray for fertility and good love matches. In January, it is much colder of course, and people have to find places indoor to couple.

"Sex Emancipation Day is the biggest and most popular festival here. But, on another part of the island, there is a Gifts of the Mountains/Gift of the Seas Festival twice year. In spring, the villagers in the mountains go down to visit the villagers near the sea. During the day, they exchange commodities, and that night they exchange wives and husbands. In autumn, the fisher folk trek to the mountain village, and the festival is repeated.

"There is also a Pussy Shrine hidden in a remote corner of the island. If you encounter someone of the opposite sex on the precincts of the shrine, you are obligated to have sex with him or her on the spot. Of course, the shrine is off the beaten path. So the only reason to go there is to have sex. There are people there every night, mostly lechers I'm afraid.

"Since you are a practitioner of the Tachikawa Ryu," the abbot continued, "I suggest that, when you go back to the main island of Honshu, you next visit the Temple of Sexual Bliss. That is the temple's secret name. Its actual name is Temple of Attaining the Way." (Dai-en wondered how the abbot knew about his Tachikawa Ryu background since he had never mentioned it.)

Dai-en was ready to move on. The abbot gave him a letter of introduction to present to the Temple of Sexual Bliss.

"They are a secretive society and do not like to be bothered by outsiders or government officials," the abbot explained. "The priest's name is Ryukoku, 'Dragon Valley.'"

Dai-en was off the next day. It took nearly a month to reach the town where the temple was located. It was a town, not a village, and the number of people Dai-en encountered was much larger than usual. But, despite the town's size, he found the temple without difficulty. It was located on the outskirts of the town.

There was nothing special about the Temple of Sexual Bliss from the outside. The buildings were nondescript. But there was a very nice Dosojin statue near the crossroads, well tended with many offerings of flowers and other gifts.

The priest Ryukoku was in. Once again, Dai-en's presence did not seem to be a surprise.

"Yes, I was informed we would have a visitor. Please come inside," said Ryukoku as he beckoned Dai-en.

A pretty young woman brought them tea and cakes.

"We are actually a Jodo Shinshu (Pure Land) temple, not Shingon," Ryukoku began. "That is why it is no problem for me to have a wife. (Jodo priests can openly marry.) However, like the Tachikawa Ryu patriarch Monkan, the founder of our school, Saint Shinran, had a vision of Kannon. Shinran had intercourse with her after she told him that he could find salvation through the embrace of a woman. There is also the example of Rennyo, the eighth Primate of our School. In his life, he had five wives and twenty-seven children, the last born when he was eighty-four years old.

"Our rites are much less complicated than those of the Tachikawa Ryu," Ryukoku continued. "These are simple farm folk with little time for abstract philosophy or time-consuming prayers. Every month we have an evening worship—a communication in mind and body among the members of the congregation and between each worshipper and Amida Buddha (the Buddha who made a vow to save every sentient being). We have about sixty families. There is room for ten couples at the nighttime worship. Any parishioner can place his or her name in bowls—one for men and one for women. A few days before the nighttime worship, I select ten names from each bowl, and I then inform the worshippers.

"It is remarkable," Ryukoku went on. "Some people get chosen nearly every time, and some people almost never. Also, some people are not interested in joining. That is fine. Once in a while, we let itinerant priests or nuns participate if they have introductions, but otherwise the nighttime worship is closed to outsiders.

"This is how the worship is conducted," Ryukoku explained. "Everyone dons a plain Amida Buddha mask and a Buddhist-style robe. The ten men and ten women line up on opposite sides of the temple hall. After facing the altar where Amida Buddha is enshrined, everyone chants *Namu Amida Butsu* (Hail to Amida Butsu) 108 times. Several large screens are placed between the men and women.

The women throw their sashes over the curtain, and each man grabs one of the sashes. The screens are removed, and people are free to have intercourse with those who hold the other end of the sash. The parishioners keep their masks on and imagine themselves sporting in the Pure Land of Amida Buddha in the West. There is no high or low there, no inferior or superior, no inequality between female and male. We are all destined to be children of Buddha. We thank Amida for this wonderful blessing that everyone can share. We believe sexual intercourse is a taste of the paradise to come.

"Even with the masks in place, it is not hard to figure out who the other person is, since we are all members of the same congregation. Again, it is peculiar how often husbands and wives get paired together even though everything is by chance. I have heard that even when that happens, the sex is much better here in the temple than at home!

"There are a few other Pure Land temples that have communal worship of this kind, and one or two are completely random—thus it is possible for brothers to end up with sisters, or fathers with daughters and mothers with sons. But I make sure that that does not happen here—it would lead to too many complications in our small group.

"After two incense sticks have burned, I sound a bell. Everyone returns to his or her original position, and we again chant the Holy Name 108 times. The men and women leave the main hall by separate entrances and return home.

"My wife and I occasionally join in," Ryukoku said in reply to Dai-en's next thought, "but we usually stay in the background and make sure things run smoothly. They almost always do.

"Would you like to participate?" Ryukoku asked generously. "We have an evening worship in a couple of days. I will select only nine male names from the bowl and include yours as the tenth."

Dai-en agreed.

The service began in the early evening. Everything proceeded as Ryukoku had described. Dai-en found himself paired with an older "Sister Buddha." (She in turn called him "Brother Buddha.") They did not know each other of course, and Sister Buddha, who mistook Dai-en's youth for inexperience, gently but firmly told him what to do. As she guided his little buddha into her lotus, she whispered, "Nine shallow and one deep stroke." Dai-en did as instructed, expertly he thought, and she quivered a bit in a few minutes.

"Now, from behind," Sister Buddha commanded. Dai-en followed her orders. "As deep as you can," she muttered. Dai-en's little buddha was hard and long, and she seemed very happy. Since Sister Buddha was in charge, Dai-en was mostly passive, letting her grind her hips and control the pace. "Oh Brother Buddha! Oh Brother Buddha!" she suddenly cried softly.

Now it was Dai-en's turn. He got on top and let himself thrust hard and fast. He shot long and abundantly in her jade gate; it was a much more intense and longer lasting bliss than he had experienced during his encounter with Haru at the Sex Emancipation Day. After a short rest in each other's arms, the bell sounded, and they returned to their places. Dai-en noticed how bright and buoyant the chanting was after the worship. Indeed, a deep sense of joy pervaded the hall.

Afterward, Dai-en thought a great deal about the differences between the Shingon and Pure Land Schools. Shingon was a doctrine for aristocrats and intellectuals; its cosmology and rites were extraordinarily complex. And, as Shingon was subtle and refined, so were the teachings and practices of the Tachikawa Ryu. He was glad that he had taken notes (in a secret code) during his training with Gessho. The correct performance of the rites, chants, and gestures of Shingon was mind-boggling. In contrast, the Pure Land teaching was the faith of ordinary people. Trust in the Vow of Amida to save you, and all will be well! Even though the sex at the nighttime worship was straightforward and uncomplicated, Dai-en had to admit that it was almost as powerful for him as Tachikawa Ryu sex, and he felt that, in the sex worship, most of the participants truly had an experience of Amida's grace.

The next day, Ryukoku told Dai-en, "On your way back to Edo, stop off at a temple located on Mount Fuji called the Fuji Mountain Sunrise Temple. It is center of the

Fuji Congregation, a group even older than the Tachikawa Ryu."

Since Dai-en had wanted to ascend Mount Fuji as part of his pilgrimage, he was glad to visit the temple as well. The temple was rather ramshackle, and the priest, named Tetsugen, was a mountain ascetic with long hair and beard.

"The Fuji Congregation is ancient," Tetsugen told Dai-en. "It existed long before Buddhism was introduced into our land. Sexual congress was believed to be the best way to worship sacred Mount Fuji. Later, after Buddhist ideas began to influence us, we said sex was the best way to express our Buddha-nature. Our approach is summed up in this text:

The human body is the universe. The eyes are the sun and moon, the senses are the stars, the limbs east and west, north and south. A man's jewel spear is the mountain, a lady's cavern is the valley. The 360 bones of the body are the days of the year. The physical body is the manifestation of universal emptiness.

The union of female and male gives birth to all life. It provides nourishment for all beings. When the body is animated, it is the abode of the gods; when the body dies it becomes a Buddha. All the gods and Buddhas are within the human form.

When a man and woman come together, it is the abode of enlightenment. The man is the pillar of heaven, the woman

Daoist Loving Couple: Your body contains mine / My body is part of yours / Together we form a perfect circle of enlightenment.

is the deep ocean. The actions of sexual congress reveal the truth.

Sexual congress is the realm of bliss. The two roots cannot be separated; they cannot exist independently. The fusion of male and female results in the creation of the universe. Learn how to generate snow (love fluid), dew (love drops), wind (bliss), and selflessness (enlightenment) through sexual congress.

The woman's jade gate is the birthplace of all the gods and Buddhas of the past, present, and future. It is the gate of life. Her womb is the inner temple of enlightenment. Her lotus is the adornment of Buddhahood. Union with a woman manifests the truth of existence (creation of a child).

Sexual congress can turn ignorance, anger, and greed into wisdom and compassion. That which comes into being will pass out of being; the existence of a human being is always perched on the edge of life and death. Sexual congress bridges the gap between life and death.

Sex is divine. Sex is the gift of the gods. Sex is magic. Sex is immortality. Sex is Buddha.

Use this teaching wisely and you will attain enlightenment in this very body; misuse it and you will burn in hell forever.

"Worshippers have to be accepted into our Fuji Congregation by unanimous consent," Tetsugen told Dai-en. "We meet once a month in a hidden cave on the mountain. Besides being within the body of the sacred mountain, the cave is cool in summer and warm in winter! The rites are simple: Short prayers to the mountain spirit, and then love-making with one's regular partner."

Dai-en could not participate since he was not a member and lacked a regular partner, but that was fine with him. He was anxious to climb the mountain and then visit the Temple of the Courtesan Buddha in another province.

On the way, Dai-en encountered a group of pilgrims, ten men and ten women who were traveling to worship at a famous Shoten temple on Mount Ikoma. The group had been on a pilgrimage to different temples and shrines. Dai-en was surprised to learn that many of the sacred places had a special *okomori* room or rooms where the male and female pilgrims could stay overnight, sleeping together like "a batch of fish" with no questions asked. In fact, the purpose of this pilgrimage was as much for sex as for worship.

"Although there are a few couples who prefer to stay together, we usually sleep with a different partner at each *okomori*," one of the female pilgrims confided. "The love-making is part of the pilgrimage, too." Dai-en later discovered that such pilgrims were common; in this case, at any rate, he felt that they were sincere in their devotion, both to the gods and Buddhas and to sex.

Dai-en also joined three Kumano nuns who were on the same road. Kumano nuns had the bad reputation of being mere prostitutes dressed up in religious habits, and most were in fact common whores. But Dai-en discovered that these Kumano nuns were followers of the Tachikawa Ryu. (They had immediately recognized him as a fellow practitioner—and, once again, Dai-en wondered how they knew.)

"We became nuns after our husbands died," the senior nun, named Marvelous Flower of the Law, said. "We kept the precepts strictly and learned all the rites. However, our husbands' families wanted nothing to do with us any more, and there is little support for nuns in this society. The abbess who first took us in and ordained us was a believer in Tachikawa Ryu teachings. She told us that we could practice Buddhism as religious courtesans—that we needed to look upon each of our customers as a fellow pilgrim along the Way and give each a taste of the Pure Land. Actually, most of the men who we meet behave well, and everyone's needs are satisfied. A couple of my partners have been *hijiri* (itinerant holy men), and one or two I really felt were enlightened. The sex with them was very powerful."

After Dai-en left the nuns, he came across one of these holy men, traveling along the same road. They chatted as they walked, and the conversation turned to sacred sex.

"In general, the *hijiri* are a bad lot," began the holy man, whose name was Yukai. "They are mostly imposters and charlatans. Many are seducers of women—or worse, outright rapists. However, although I have never made advances toward any female, I am often visited at night by the wife, daughter, or even grandmother of the house I am staying in." (Dai-en had noticed how attractive Yukai was; the holy man's gaze was especially penetrating.)

"On occasion, a family will ask me to sleep with a homely, diseased, or crippled daughter. I do so willingly and with care and tenderness. I have journeyed all over this land, and made love with hundreds of women—young and old, pretty and plain, healthy and sick, rich and poor. I never discriminate. I see each one as a bodhisattva, a potential Buddha."

Dai-en finally reached the Temple of the Courtesan Buddha. It was small but tidy, with one resident priest.

"About a hundred years ago," the priest began, "an extraordinarily beautiful courtesan suddenly appeared in the village. Everyone believed that she had escaped from her confinement in the pleasure quarters in the capital and had come here to hide. Several of the men accosted her of course, but she was kind to each one, and gave them want they wanted. But the men were completely transformed by their encounters with her—one gave up drinking, another stopped abusing his wife and children, another stopped gambling. The villagers set her up in a little house, and she saw a steady stream of male visitors. She took whatever they offered her, and she made love to all sweetly. Every single man changed for the better, and a few were completely reformed, becoming generous patrons of the poor or outstanding monks.

"But, alas, she died suddenly a few months after turning up in the village. The fragrance that wafted from her house after she died was delectable, and the room where she was lying in repose seemed to radiate. The villagers decided to enshrine her in this temple. Rumor has it that she was really an incarnation of Kannon, the Goddess of Compassion. Many pilgrims still come here today to honor her spirit, and cures of diseases of the heart or body are often reported."

DAI-EN DECIDED TO return to his home temple. Kakusho was still abbot, older of course but remarkably spry. He welcomed Dai-en back, and they talked much about his Tachikawa Ryu experiences. Dai-en knew, though, that his training was incomplete. He had never forgotten Lady Hotoke, and, with Kakusho's blessing, he decided to seek her out.

Hotoke was still at the same residence. She had been practicing Zen meditation diligently in the mornings while Dai-en had been training and traveling. During the day, she gave lessons in tea ceremony and koto to a few courtesans and some samurai wives and daughters.

Hotoke was surprised to discover Dai-en in the entranceway when she went to see who was calling. She had never forgotten him. He looked well but rather sunburnt from his long pilgrimage. Since Hotoke had a student at the time, she asked Dai-en to come back later when she was free.

Hotoke told Dosen about Dai-en's return and confessed what had occurred between them.

"Now he is back, and I agreed to see him," she said.

"I think that is fine," Dosen said. "Perhaps you have found a partner who will engage you in 'couple Zen.' As you have discovered, *zazen* is a solitary pursuit—it is you with the universe as a reference. For real understanding of Zen, however, you need a flesh-and-blood *koan* (conundrum) to work with, a human being to share your practice."

Dosen always had a brush, ink, and paper ready. He dashed off a Zen painting of a couple making love and added this inscription:

> *This is the original form of integration with the cosmos,*
> *A Buddhist practice to harmonize the two roots;*
> *Naked, climb the opposite peak*
> *And achieve non-dual union.*

He gave the painting to Hotoke.

When Dai-en came to visit Hotoke, they recounted their respective adventures. Dai-en had traveled all over the country; Hotoke had roamed the mountains of her mind. Both were far more mature and seasoned now due to their respective modes of training. Not surprisingly, they came together as a couple. The passion was just as intense as the first time, but their love-making was much more controlled and refined.

Dai-en left the monastery and gave up wearing his robes. He moved in with Lady Hotoke. One of the skills he had picked up in the temples of Shikoku was divination—actually, he had become a skillful reader of minds and interpreter of dreams. He soon had a devoted following, and he made a living by fortune telling.

Dai-en shared his Tachikawa Ryu teachings with Hotoke; she taught him Zen meditation. They had children. Eventually, after many years together, they went to live and teach at Wago Shrine.

All Hail!

Tachikawa Ryu loving couple in Shinto dress.

Note

THIS ACCOUNT OF the Tantra of the Tachikawa Ryu is based on actual events, real historical figures, and authentic Tantric tradition in Japan. Like all Tantric texts, it is condensed and cryptic; it needs to be augmented by oral instruction. Tantra is a living tradition, adapting itself to time, place, and social conditions. Old texts will fade away to be replaced by new ones in a different idiom but still rooted in the Tantric experience. May many new and original Tantric texts be composed in English and other modern languages to become an integral part of world culture!

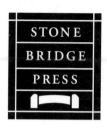